WILLIAM MORRIS
An Arts & Crafts Coloring Book

William Morris: An Arts & Crafts Coloring Book © 2016 Victoria and Albert Museum, London/Thames & Hudson Ltd, London

Text and V&A images © 2016 Victoria and Albert Museum, London
Line illustrations © 2016 Thames & Hudson Ltd, London
Line illustrations by Carissa Chan

First published in 2016 in paperback in the United States of America by Thames & Hudson Inc., 500 Fifth Avenue, New York, New York 10110

thamesandhudsonusa.com

Library of Congress Catalog Card Number 2016941854

ISBN 978-0-500-42059-1

Printed and bound in China by Reliance Printing (Shen Zhen) Co., Ltd

WILLIAM MORRIS

An Arts & Crafts Coloring Book

Thames & Hudson | V&A

INTRODUCTION

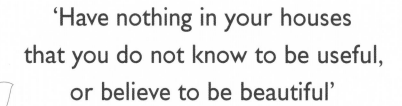

'Have nothing in your houses
that you do not know to be useful,
or believe to be beautiful'

William Morris

WILLIAM MORRIS (24 March 1834—3 October 1896) was a textile designer, artist, writer, socialist, and a key figure in the English Arts and Crafts movement. His innovative designs, initially made only for his own use, but later developed by his company Morris & Co., are still manufactured and sold today.

Red House in southeast London, where Morris lived from 1860, is now owned by the National Trust and is open to the public. It contains original furnishings and artworks created by Morris and by his friends and collaborators, painter Edward Burne-Jones and architect Philip Webb. Although some early visitors to Red House found its highly patterned and richly coloured design scheme curious, many others admired the original furnishings and wanted to use them in their own homes.

Morris established his own workshops in central and south London in 1861. Morris & Co. aimed to improve the standards of decorative design in Britain, as well as the conditions under which it was manufactured. The company designed products including stained-glass windows, furniture, decorated tiles, printed and woven textiles, furnishing, carpets and tapestries. These were sold at the Morris & Co. shop on Oxford Street, London, and in major cities throughout Europe, America and Australia. The company ceased trading in 1941, but Morris & Co. designs still decorate homes worldwide.

Morris saw no conflict between his work as an artist and his role as an entrepreneur. He believed that true artistic quality and commercial success could go hand-in-hand because he trusted the public to recognize beauty and skilled craftsmanship. His rare talent for creating original and beautiful combinations of pattern and colour was underpinned by thorough study of traditional pattern formations and historical textiles. His research and exacting standards were acclaimed in his lifetime, and he advised institutions including the Victoria and Albert Museum (then called the South Kensington Museum).

The V&A holds an extensive collection of wallpapers, textiles and tile designs by Morris & Co., and the patterns in this book are selected from that collection. Here they can be coloured in to personal taste and kept as unique decorative works. The originals can be viewed in the galleries and study rooms of the V&A and online at www.vam.ac.uk.

NATURE

'The rose, the lily, the tulip, the oak,
the vine, and all the herbs and trees that
even we cockneys know about … '

William Morris

Morris designs demonstrate an authority gained from close observation of natural forms. His patterns feature flowers, trees, insects, birds and animals studied from the world around him, but when he began designing in the 1860s, his choice of indigenous British flora was highly unusual. Brightly coloured, exotic, and thus usually imported blooms were considered the only acceptable floral decoration for the home at the time. Morris introduced a new design language to interior furnishing, inspired by local field and hedgerow plants, such as columbine, larkspur, fritillary and honeysuckle. Branches of oak, willow and acanthus leaves usually provided the structure in which the floral motifs would sit.

'Those natural forms which are at once most familiar and most delightful to us, as well from association as from beauty, are the best for our purpose', Morris wrote. One of his first wallpaper designs, 'Trellis', was inspired by rose trellises in the courtyard of his home,

Red House. The birds in this early design were drawn by Morris's collaborator and friend, Philip Webb. Morris used the pattern, on a blue ground, for the wallpaper in a room that overlooked his garden. The pattern enhanced the close connection between outdoor and indoor space. This connection to nature became a guiding principle of Arts and Crafts buildings, in which architects and designers sought to leave the small, dark rooms of earlier periods behind, and create light and airy spaces opening out on to gardens.

Morris was also inspired by his travels in Northern France, Iceland, and Germany — sending back letters full of observations on the landscapes and wildlife around him. He was acutely aware that industrialization and urban development posed a risk to natural environments everywhere. In his later years, he campaigned publicly to preserve the countryside.

COLOUR

'I never met a man who understood so much about colours'

Sir Thomas Wardle, silk dyer,
about William Morris

As a student, Morris developed a passion for medieval art that shaped the course of his career. After visiting the cathedrals of northern France with Edward Burne-Jones, both men decided to quit their studies and begin 'a life of art'. Morris loved the 'crispness and abundance of detail' he found in medieval art and, above all, its rich colours. Deep blues and reds feature repeatedly within the wide and varied colour palette of Morris & Co. designs.

In his quest to reproduce the colours of historical textiles, Morris abandoned contemporary manufacturing practices and revived older vegetable printing and dyeing techniques. In 1875 he began to experiment with indigo blue and madder red, among other coloured dyes, in collaboration with Thomas Wardle at his print works in Staffordshire. Wardle said of Morris, 'I never met a man who understood so much about colours'.

The search for a perfect indigo blue occupied Morris over several years. He finally perfected the process of indigo dyeing and discharge printing in 1881 when he established his own textile factory at Merton Abbey on the River Wandle. The patterns 'Rose and Thistle', 'Brother Rabbit', 'Wandle' and 'Lodden' were all produced there. Morris was typically dressed in a baggy suit of blue

serge, with an indigo dyed shirt of brighter blue. His handkerchiefs would also invariably be blue, having been used to demonstrate the workings of the indigo vat.

Morris was insistent that the colours of his designs should be matched precisely in the finished products. He entrusted his wallpaper designs to printers Jeffrey & Co. with strict instructions, 'not to improve my colourings'. The design 'Acanthus' (1874) incorporates 15 different colours and was printed in a number of different colourways. Complex designs like this pushed the technical skills of his printers to the limit. By the end of the 1870s, the Morris & Co. wallpaper range included 32 different patterns in 125 different colourways.

Letters from Morris to his clients reveal the passionate and detailed attention he gave to colour choices, '[this] madder printed cotton brings out the greys of the picture better than anything else: also I think it would make a pretty room with the woodwork painted a light green-blue colour like a starling's egg; and if you wanted drapery about it, we have beautiful shades of red that would brighten all up without fighting with the wall-hangings'. Morris & Co. set a lasting fashion for creative, considered, colourful interior design.

MORRIS & CO., L.

No. ....1351......

Name...Bird & Aneu-

Width.........36 in....

Price......4/- per yard.

'The workman [is] not the brainless 'hand' but the intelligent co-operator … '

William Morris

Morris set exactingly high standards of craftsmanship for his company and subcontractors. He insisted on learning himself how things were made and was involved on a personal, practical, level in all the manufacturing processes of Morris & Co., from weaving to embroidery. He selected old manufacturing techniques such as block printing and hand weaving that he identified in the historical pieces he admired. Intricately carved woodblocks were used to print complex designs such as Morris's iconic 'Strawberry Thief' and others including 'Iris', 'Compton' and 'Cray'. The latter required the largest number of blocks of any Morris design.

Morris attempted to follow and revive medieval techniques not because he was backward-looking and entrenched in tradition, but because he had looked at contemporary practice and found it unable to produce the beauty he wanted. Despite the high value he placed on handcraft skills, from wood-carving to embroidery, he was ready to use machine-manufacturing techniques and mass-produce his designs where this could be done without a loss of quality: he not only revived the historical techniques he needed but also devised new ones. 'Granada', the most expensive of all Morris fabrics at £10 a yard, was made of silk velvet brocaded in gold thread, and a special loom was built to produce it in 1884 at Merton Abbey. Morris saw the value of such experimentation but, in the event, conceded that the production process was too expensive to be commercially viable.

The value Morris placed on craftsmanship was reflected in his treatment of his company employees. To an American visitor he set out his view that workers should be given a healthy working environment, fair pay, protection in the case of sickness or trouble, and respect: 'the workman … shall be made to feel himself not the brainless 'hand' but the intelligent co-operator, the friend of the man who directs his labour'.

PATTERN

'Do not be afraid of large patterns …
a pattern where the structure is large
and the details much broken up
is the most useful'

William Morris

Morris had a natural eye for pattern, combined with an ability to see designs as masses of shape and colour instead of a series of lines. He trained his eye through extensive study of historical textiles and designs. One of his earliest patterns, 'Daisy', referenced a motif found in a medieval French manuscript in the British Museum. The free-flowing diagonal movement of his design 'Fruit' was inspired by Byzantine patterns, which Morris admired for their 'continuous line'. The diagonal lines in a piece of seventeenth-century Italian cut velvet seen by Morris at the V&A inspired a series of designs including 'Evenlode' and 'Wey'. Morris immersed himself in collections of Italian, Persian and Turkish textiles.

Morris also responded to nineteenth-century trends and styles. In the late 1870s imported Indian silks became highly fashionable in Britain, and Morris created a group of Eastern-inspired patterns featuring small, square or diaper motifs — 'Indian Diaper', 'Snakeshead',
'Little Chintz' and 'Pomegranate'. Having found patterns that inspired him, Morris freely adapted them and made them his own. He brought distinctive motifs and subjects into interior design, drawn from English nature, and developed his own original palette. His patterns were instantly recognizable, distinctive and daring for the time.

While some of his contemporaries sold designs to manufacturers for any usage, Morris insisted that patterns should be designed with specific materials, production techniques and settings in mind. Several of his patterns were adapted when they were transferred, for example, from a textile to a wallpaper or tile. Morris & Co. also developed bespoke patterns to commission for distinctive buildings and settings; from the restaurant of the V&A, to grand homes such as Membland Hall or St James's Palace. The 'Green Dining Room' Morris & Co. created for the V&A is still enjoyed by visitors to the café today.

CAPTIONS

'Tulip and Willow', 1873
Designed by William Morris,
produced by Morris & Co. after 1883
Printed linen
V&A: CIRC.91—1933

Tapestry design with peacocks, 1879—81
Designed by William Morris
Pencil and bodycolour on paper
V&A: E.620—1939

'Trellis', 1862
Designed by William Morris,
produced by Morris & Co., 1864
Woodblock print on paper
V&A: E.452—1919

'Rose' textile design, 1883
Designed by William Morris
Pencil, pen and ink, watercolour
on paper
V&A: E.1075—1988

'Honeysuckle', 1876
Designed by William Morris,
produced for Morris & Co.
Block-printed cotton
V&A: CIRC.196—1934

'Willow Bough', 1887
Designed by William Morris,
produced by Morris & Co.
Block-printed on paper
V&A: E.558—1919

'The Forest' tapestry (detail), 1887
Designed by William Morris, Philip Webb
and John Henry Dearle
Woven wool and silk
V&A: T.111—1926

'Vine' wallpaper design, 1873
Designed by William Morris
Pencil and watercolour on paper
V&A: E.1074—1988

Tile, 1872—80
Designed by William Morris,
decorated by the firm of
William De Morgan
Hand-painted in blue and green on
tin-glazed earthenware tile
V&A: C.220—1976

'Blackthorn'
Designed by John Henry Dearle,
produced by Morris & Co. from
1882—96
Woodblock print on paper
V&A: E.602—1919

'Pomegranate', 1877
Designed by William Morris,
produced by Morris & Co.
Printed onto cotton and tusser silk
V&A: T.592—1919

'Rose and Thistle' textile design, 1882
Designed by William Morris
Charcoal and watercolour on paper
V&A: E.293—1939

'Acanthus' wallpaper design, 1874
Designed by William Morris,
produced by Morris & Co.
Pencil, watercolour and bodycolour
on paper
V&A: CIRC.297—1955

'Peacock and Dragon', 1878
Designed by William Morris,
produced by Morris & Co.
Hand-loom jacquard-woven woollen
twill, with braid trimmings
V&A: T.64—1933

'Brother rabbit' (or 'Brer Rabbit'),
1880—81
Designed by William Morris,
produced by Morris & Co.
Printed cotton
V&A: T.648—1919

'Wandle', 1884
Designed by William Morris,
produced by Morris & Co.
Printed cotton
V&A: T.45—1912

'Bird and Anemone', 1900—10
Designed by William Morris,
John Henry Dearle and Kate Faulkner
Swatch sample from a book of
58 pieces of block-printed
cottons and linen
V&A: T.34—1982

'Utrecht Velvet', 1871
Retailed by Morris, Marshall,
Faulkner & Co.
Stamped and dyed woollen plush
V&A: T.210—1953

'Snakeshead', 1876
Designed by Morris,
produced by Thomas Wardle & Co.
Block-printed cotton
V&A: T.37—1919

'Acanthus' fabric, 1875
Designed by William Morris,
produced by Morris & Co.
Hand-loom jacquard-woven woollen
twill, with braid trimmings
V&A: CIRC.7A—1966

'Lodden', 1883
Designed by William Morris,
produced by Morris & Co.
Block-printed cotton
V&A: T.39—1919

'The Artichoke' embroidery design,
about 1877
Designed by William Morris
Pencil and watercolour on paper
V&A. 65—1898

'Strawberry Thief', 1883
Designed by William Morris,
produced by Morris & Co.
Printed cotton
V&A: T.586—1919

'Compton' wallpaper, 1896
Designed by William Morris,
produced by Morris & Co.
Woodblock print on paper
V&A: E.607—1919

'Flowerpot' embroidery design, 1878—80
Designed by William Morris,
embroidered by May Morris
Silk embroidery on wool
V&A: T.68—1939

'Granada', 1884
Designed by William Morris,
produced by Morris & Co.
Woven silk velvet brocaded with
gold thread
V&A: T.4—1919

'Cray', 1884
Designed by William Morris,
produced by Morris & Co.
Printed cotton
V&A: T.34—1919

'Iris' wallpaper, about 1887
Designed by John Henry Dearle
for Morris & Co.
Woodblock print on paper
V&A: E.699—1915

'The Artichoke' wall hanging, 1877—1900
Designed by William Morris,
embroidered by Ada Godman
Wool embroidery on linen
V&A: T.166—1978

Italian cut velvet, 1500—1600
Designed in Genoa, owned by
William Morris
Cut and uncut silk velvet on a ground
brocaded with gold thread
V&A: 442A—1883

The Bullerswood Carpet, 1889
Designed by William Morris and
probably John Henry Dearle,
made by Morris & Co.
Hand-knotted woollen pile on a
cotton warp
V&A: T.31—1923

Tile panel, 1876
Designed by William Morris,
decorated by the firm of
William De Morgan
Slip-covered and hand-painted
earthenware
V&A: C.36—1972

'Indian Diaper', 1875
Designed by William Morris,
produced by Morris & Co.
Printed cotton
V&A: T.585—1919

'Indian', about 1868—70
Designed by William Morris,
produced by Morris & Co.
Woodblock print on paper
V&A: E.3707—1927

'Fruit' or 'Pomegranate', about 1866
Designed by William Morris,
produced by Morris & Co.
Woodblock printed on paper
V&A: E.447—1919

'Madras', 1880—81
Designed by William Morris,
produced by Morris & Co.
Woven cotton and silk leno (gauze)
V&A: T.657—1919

'Evenlode' textile design, 1883
Designed by William Morris
Black chalk and bodycolour on paper
V&A: E.543—1939

'Daisy', about 1868—70
Designed by William Morris,
produced by Morris & Co.
Woodblock print on paper
V&A: E.3720—1927

Design for the decoration of the Green
Dining Room, South Kensington Museum,
1866—7
Designed by Philip Webb and
William Morris
Pencil, charcoal and watercolour on a
sheet collaged from two pieces of paper
V&A: E.1169—1940

'Wey', about 1883
Designed by William Morris,
produced by Morris & Co.
Printed cotton
V&A: T.49—1912

This book draws on the analysis of William Morris by
Linda Parry and Lucia van der Post in the following titles:

Linda Parry, *William Morris Textiles* (V&A Publishing: 2013)
and *V&A Pattern: William Morris* (V&A Publishing: 2009)
Lucia van der Post, *William Morris and Morris & Co.*
(V&A Publishing: 2003)